THE COMET AND OTHER VERSES

THE COMET AND OTHER VERSES

IRVING SIDNEY DIX

ISBN: 978-93-5614-085-1

Published: -

LECTOR HOUSE LLP
E-MAIL: lectorpublishing@gmail.com

THE COMET AND OTHER VERSES

BY

IRVING SIDNEY DIX

DEDICATION

To the Memory of my school mate William Morgan who was drowned in the Delaware.

WITH THE READER

It should be stated that some of these verses, in a slightly different form, have previously appeared in various periodicals in Binghamton, Scranton, Philadelphia and New York City, but most of them appear here for the first time, and also, perhaps it should be mentioned that some of these stanzas were written during my school days. However, the majority of the following verses have been composed since the former booklet was published.

And if in any way you have been helped to see, that even here in this rugged country "the poetry of earth is never ceasing," however rude my interpretation of it may seem to the critical, the labor and expense of publishing this little volume will be fully justified.

Irving Dix.

FOREWORD

A few years ago, while recovering from an illness, I conceived the idea of writing some reminiscent lines on country life in the Wayne Highlands. And during the interval of a few days I produced some five hundred couplets,—a few good, some bad and many indifferent—and such speed would of necessity invite the indifferent. A portion of these lines were published in 1907. However, I had hoped to revise and republish them, with additions of the same type, at a later date as a souvenir volume of verses for those who spend the summer months among these hills—as well as for the home-fast inhabitants. But in substituting the following collection of verses I hope my judgment will be confirmed by those who chance to read these simple stanzas of one, who—

> "Loves not man the less, but Nature more
> From those our interviews, in which I steal
> From all I may be or have been before,
> To mingle with the Universe and feel
> What I can ne'er express, yet cannot all conceal."

I. S. D.

CONTENTS

THE COMET

Swift circuit-rider of the endless skies,
Thou wanderer of the outer, unknown air,
Amid those dim, uncharted regions there,
Imagination droops—in deep surprise
Man doth behold thee, and the fearful speed
At which thou spurrest on thy flaming steed.

Born of the dark and ever-deepening Past,
Who nurs'd thee there in yonder viewless space
Afar from earth—thy all-beholding face
Hath gazed unspeakable, with clear eye cast
Worldward on each magnificent return
As if of human progress thou wouldst learn.

And thou hast seen each triumph and each plan
By which the human race since human time
Hath learned at last Earth's secrets all-sublime
While rising from the elements to man—
Hast seen it triumph over sea and air
And universal knowledge hope to share.

Thy circuit measures well the age of man,
The epoch of a life—and few there be
Who seeing thee, thy face again may see,
For human life is but a little span,
With varying cycles of a different day,
And in diffusion wears itself away.

Child of the Sun, when first the human eye
Beheld thee coursing in the night afar
Like an illumined spectre of a star—
Beheld thy awful form against the sky
Strong men fell earthward with a coward-cry
On their pale lips, as if afraid to die—

And that brute King—Nero, the cruel King,
When looking on thy fiery face unknown,
Sate trembling on his little human throne,
And thought that thou didst evil tidings bring—
That thou wert writing on the distant skies

A doom from which no human king could rise.

Thy age is all unknown—man can but guess
The time when first the Sun thy circle set—
He can but guess thy secret birth—and yet
Observing thee his knowledge is not less;
He knows each cycle, each return to be
A moment in that vast eternity.

Recording-comet of th' immortal space,
What history thy eye hath look'd upon
Since first thy airy, circling course was run!
What fallen pride! What scatterings of race!
Jerusalem and Nineveh and Rome
Didst thou behold from thy almighty dome—

Didst thou behold—their birth, their rise, their fall—
Low humbled by the under hordes at last,
With glory and fair triumphs in the past,
And footprints of destruction over all.
While thou, fleet comet, with a light divine
Continueth upon the earth to shine.

Speed on! swift comet—turn, wanderer, turn!
And with thy flaming, god-like pen of light
On heaven's scroll with burning letters write:
Live but to love, O earth!—to love and learn,
For while a comet's mighty cycles fail,
Love,—love and truth forever shall prevail.

WASHINGTON

It is forever so—when there is need
Of some clear, clarion voice to forward lead
God raiseth up a man from his own seed;
Not from the soft, luxurious lap of earth,
But from a nobler soil, so that from birth
The frame is moulded with a chosen food
That has one only end—to make it good,
Full generous, far-sighted, firm and keen,
With strength to rise above the gross and mean—
The sordid selfishness that like a curse
Drives from the heart the virtues it would nurse—
That love of country, freedom's holy cause,
Justice, mercy, that eye for equal laws,
Faith in the future and our fellow-men,
Faith in the sword when shielded by the pen—
And so it was with us—when there was need
Of one commanding voice to forward lead,
God rais'd up here a man from His own seed;
And so came forth the gentle Washington,
Fair child of Fate, the nation's noblest son,
Whom Virtue fostered and whom Virtue won.

Some few there be whose feet knew rougher ground,
But few indeed a loftier summit found—
Nurtured in tender soil, he held a path
Where others faltered, heeding not the wrath
Of any king or potentate or power—
His was the hero-heart—he saw the hour,—
He knew the mighty odds, yet would not cower.
And when the tyrant's heel touch'd on our shore
And thrust itself unbidden to our door,—
But Washington alone with eagle-eye
Withstood the foe and taught him how to die;
Repulsed, disheartened, driven to despair,
He lifted up his voice in humble prayer,
For in that awful night at Valley Forge
He drank the bitter cup—he knew Fate's scourge,
He felt her lash,—this tender-hearted George.

Father of Liberty—thou Child of Light,
Columbia's first-born, who in thy might
Restored to Freedom her enfeebled sight—
If spirits of the nobler dead can hear,
This day—thy natal day—press close thine ear
And learn what we thy nation need to fear,
And if the immortal dead can truly speak,
Show us, O Child of Light, where we are weak,—
Grant us thy counsel (for thou art with God)
And bear us wisdom where thy footsteps trod,
And if thou seest aught of envious strife
From virtue sapping all her sweeter life,
Teach us, O Child of Light, a purer love,
For thou hast learn'd of God—thou art above
Thy weak and erring mortals here below
Who see the light, yet forward fear to go—
Guide us, if spirits of the dead may guide,
So that in peace we ever may abide,
So that from land to sea, from shore to shore,
We shall be brothers now and evermore.

THE STORM

All day long the sky was cloudless,
Life was waiting for a breath,
And the heat was more oppressive
Than the fear of sudden death;
All day long the sun was shining
In a hot and windless sky,
And the trees were weak for water—
Earth and air were dead and dry.

But e'er Night her wings had folded
Came a welcome western breeze,
Moving idly through the forest,
Prophesying to the trees,
Till above that dim horizon
Giant clouds like warring foes
Marshalled far in battle numbers
As the wild winds wilder rose.

Hark! O hear the double rumble
As the thunder shakes the air,
Like a thousand hoofs advancing
In yon cloudy corral there!—
Look!—how red the lightning flashes!
How the echoes roll and roll—
Dirges from some demon goddess—
How the bells of heaven toll!

Like a lance, a flash of lightning
Cuts the foremost cloud in twain
And the thunder's mighty echo
Rolls athwart the drenching rain
Till the landscape fades like shadows
In the driving sheets of spray,
And the wind wails through the forest,
And the great trees rock and sway.

Soon the air is strangely solemn
And the winds no longer blow
To the thunder's distant drumming
In the valley far below;

And along the low horizon
All the clouds are growing dim,
While upon the western hilltops
Rolls again the sun's red rim.

And away across the valley
In the heavens arching high,
Like a bed for fairy flowers
Swings the rainbow in the sky—
Swings until the shadows gather
And the sun sinks out of sight,
Seemingly to whisper softly
To the world a fond good night.

JIM, THE NEWSBOY

Jim, the newsboy, died today,
So the evening papers say—
And the funeral will be
In the afternoon at three—
"Please" (the papers say) "a flow'r
Bring for Jim before the hour—
Any color that you deem
A true token of esteem,
If you would remember him—
The newsboy, Jim.

At his corner near Broad street,
Jim, tho' lame, would smiling greet
With a merry, winning call
All his patrons, great and small,
And his fellow newsboys say
That they miss him much today,
And they have a tablet bought,
And upon it this is wrought:
"In memory of Newsboy Jim,
We all liked him."

Little toilers on Life's road
To yon visionless abode,
There was much of good in Jim
Or the boys had disliked him;
There was something in his heart
That drew patrons to his mart,
Something noble, something true—
Strive that it be said of you
As in eulogy of Jim,
"We all liked him."

MARCH WIND BLOW

Bitter March-wind, blow and blow;
Drive away the drifting snow;
Toss the tree-tops to and fro;
Kiss the ice-bound lakes and streams
And arouse them from their dreams.

Happy March-wind, blithely blow,
Winter's heart is full of woe,
Winter's head is lying low;
Bring, O bring the melting rain
Back unto the earth again.

Weeping March-wind, blow and blow
Till thy tears of sorrow flow
Down thy dying cheeks of snow—
Weep away! for man must wait
Till those tearful winds abate.

Merry March-wind, softer blow,
Let the little children know
Where the sweetest flowers grow;
Let thy tender accents ring
From the joyous harp of Spring.

All ye wild-winds, blow and blow,
Drive away the drifting snow,
Bend the bushes, bend them low;
Breathe upon the trembling sod
Springtime's messages from God.

THE RIME OF THE RAFTMEN

I

The Delaware above the Rift
Each bank is fast o'erflowing,
And sweeping onward dark and swift,
Wild and still wilder growing
It hurls a heavy raft along
Upon its rocking way,
While the Captain's call the hills prolong
At dawning of the day:
Pull, lads, pull! — to Jersey side,
The Rift is near!
Pull, lads, pull! — for the high floods hide
The ragged rocks like an ocean tide,
And the river's rush I hear.

II

Safely the Rift is left behind,
A careful stearsman stearing;
Swiftly we speed, only to find
A dizzy eddy nearing,
Where rolling in the river-lake,
And whirling round and round
A dozen rafts the circle make,
And warning cries resound:
Pull, lads, pull! — Sylvania's shore!
The Eddy's near!
Pull, lads, pull! — till the sweeping oar
Bends like a bow and you hear the roar
Of the river in the rear.

III

The luring eddy lies behind
Where the dizzy rafts are whirling,
And we speed along with the cutting wind,
The foam like suds up-curling,
When ahead a sharp curve comes in sight

And we hear the Captain call
As the raft swerves sudden to the right
And the ridges tower tall:
Pull, lads, pull!—to Jersey side!
The Bend I fear!
Pull, lads, pull!—and soon we'll ride
On the rolling wave to Trenton's tide
With river calm and clear.

IV

The Bend is past, but the Water-gap
Of the Delaware up-rearing,
Looms far ahead like a narrow trap
As fast our raft is nearing,
And calm and deep the waters grow,
And scarcely comes a sound
Till the Captain's calling, to and fro
Re-echoes far around:
Rest, lads, rest!—a little while!
Be of good cheer!
Rest, lads, rest! till yonder isle
We safely pass—a few more mile
And all our course is clear.

V

Along the wave we smoothly glide
Until the island clearing,
When down we speed as with the tide,
Now here, now there a veering,
Until a great bridge lifts its form
Against the evening sky,
When like the rolling of a storm
The crew repeats the cry:
Pull, lads, pull!—Sylvania's shore!
The Bridge is near!
Pull, lads, pull!—the for'ard oar,
And soon our dangerous task is o'er,
And little need we fear.

VI

So on we speed; now fast, now slow;
By isle and rift and eddy
Until at length along we flow
With movement firm and steady;
And low and lower lie the hills,

And wider spreads the vale,
And soft the Captain's calling trills
Upon the evening gale:
Rest, lads, rest!—our work is done—
The danger's o'er!
Rest, lads, rest!—another sun
Will see a haven safely won
By Trenton's friendly shore.

A CHILD'S ELEGY

We know her not whom once we knew,
Who died it seems e'er death was due—
We know her not; she is asleep;
Our hearts are dumb—we can but weep
That one so young must bid adieu,
Must part so soon from earthly view.

Those tender feet we knew so late
We hear no more; we can but wait
To hear them in the House of God
When dust to dust we tread the sod,
For in that home of homes they wait
For us beside the city's gate.

Those little hands out-held in love,
That in such innocence did move
To fondle each familiar face
Are still—they cannot now embrace
As once they did so like a dove
That weary parents would approve.

Those little lips that met our own
So sweetly when we were alone
No more shall meet the lips of earth,
Sealed up unto another birth;
But when these larger lives have flown
Our lips will meet; she will be known.

Springtime was here—the birds would soon
Have re-appeared—the birds would soon
Have warbled from a new-built nest,
Would soon have felt beneath their breast
The little ones—and such a boon
Had taught them still a sweeter tune.

But of the little ones not all
Will answer to the parent-call,
Not all will learn to rise and fly—
Many are born, but some must die;
Many will rise, but some must fall,
And God knows best for each and all.

This is the hope—we know not how—
This is the hope that lures us now,
That makes the parting less of pain—
The hope that we shall meet again,
And so while unto grief we bow
The road beyond seems brighter now.

DREAMING OF THE DELAWARE

I

I have been far away from the Delaware's shore,
From the river where once I did play,
But I'm dreaming tonight by the old cottage door
Where the moonlight is gleaming bright as day.

Refrain:

Dreaming, dreaming, dreaming of that dear old stream,
Dreaming of the days that are no more—
The days so bright and fair,
Dreaming in the moonlight gleaming on the shore
Of the dear old Delaware.

II

And the river is still, and so peaceful tonight
That its murmur I scarcely can hear,
And across it the moonlight is beaming so bright
That the scenes of my childhood appear.

III

And I think of my mother who bade me farewell
And the sister who kist me good-bye—
They are sleeping below in that beautiful dell
But methinks that again they are nigh.

IV

Long deserted has been the old river home,
My old home by the dear Delaware,
But never, O never again will I roam
From the scenes of my childhood so fair.

V

I will cherish the dreams I am dreaming tonight,
Will upbuild the old homestead once more,

And perhaps when I'm dead, for another's delight
It will bloom by the Delaware's shore.

REFRAIN.

NORMA

A LEGEND OF THE WAYNE HIGHLANDS

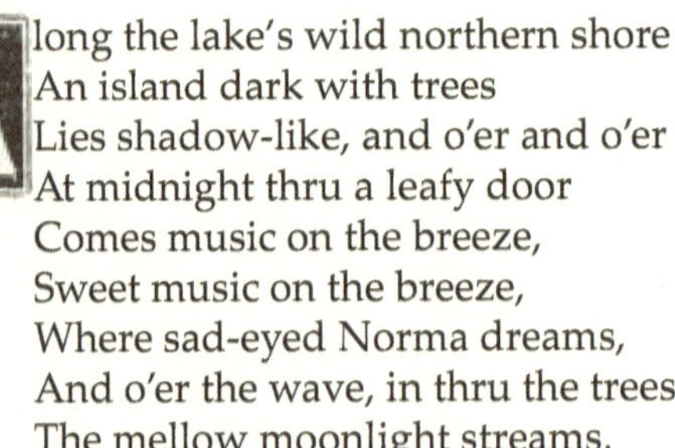

Along the lake's wild northern shore
An island dark with trees
Lies shadow-like, and o'er and o'er
At midnight thru a leafy door
Comes music on the breeze,
Sweet music on the breeze,
Where sad-eyed Norma dreams,
And o'er the wave, in thru the trees
The mellow moonlight streams.

And Norma's voice is sweet to hear
As the breathing of a bell;
But while so welcome to the ear
Of any one afar or near,
The notes, O few can tell!
The notes, O few can tell!
Falling so wildly sweet,
Like the mournful ringing of a bell
With the tones still incomplete.

How came this maid upon the isle
Within the Hills of Wayne?
Why sings she sweetly all the while
As if to ease her self-denial?
Why sings she a refrain
At the lonely midnight hour
On an island dark with trees,
Enchanting souls unto her bower
By such sweet melodies?

The legend runs:—That long ago
A lover came to woo,
But left her—why?—(no man doth know)
For while her love like wine did flow
Away from her he drew—
He drew from her away,
While she was left forlorn

And ever (so the legends say)
Did daily for him mourn.

But Norma left her home one night
When all were fast asleep
And angel-like she trod the light
Moonpath across the waters bright
Until she ceased to weep,
Until she ceased to weep,
Singing a sweet, sweet song
That on the lake that lay asleep
The night-wind did prolong.

And after Norma's death, one day
A knock at her father's door
Announced the lad who went away
When both were lovers young and gay,
Who now would love her more
Than any other maid,
Yes, any other maid,
Saying, O where is Norma now,
Where is my sweetheart now?

O Youth, my daughter is not here—
She waited, waited long
To hear the voice she held more dear
Than all the rest—nor could we cheer
Her with another song;
But many hear her sing
By the island,—sing so sweet
That never, never can they bring
The song to me complete.

The lover sadly turned away
And vowed that he would know
The song complete e'er dawn of day
And followed where the moonpath lay
Upon the lake below,
Where Norma sang of love
On the island dark with trees
That cast deep shadows on the cove,
And his heart was ill at ease.

At midnight o'er the moonlit wave
He bent his little boat,
Till he heard the song the soft winds gave,
But if his life that song might save,
He could not tell a note!
He could not learn a note!

Tho' many, and many, and many a night
In the lovely moonpath gleaming bright
He listened from his boat.

But the song he never, never knew
Altho' he listened long,
And so it is—is ever true
When hearts withhold a love long due;
For Love sings one sweet song,
One sweet familiar song,
At thy heart's door today,
And knocking, waits, but waiting long
Forever turns away.

PLANT A TREE

The Past unto the Present cries—
Arise, ye more than blind, arise!
For I who fell the forest low
Would now another forest grow,
But what is done I cannot mend,
So unto you a message send—
Much did I do for you, for me
Plant a tree,
Plant a tree.

The Present, waking from its sleep,
Across the hills began to creep,
And saw where Past had fallen far
A noble forest, with a scar
On many a wounded mountain side
That from the elements would hide—
And answered:—Past, I will for thee
Plant a tree,
A forest tree.

The feeling Future, yet unborn,
Heard Present echoing her horn,
And stirring somewhat in Life's cell
Did try her dearest wish to tell,
Whispering in an undertone:
I—I shall reap as ye have sown,
O heed the Past! and—thanks to thee—
Plant a tree,
Plant a tree.

MAID OF SHEHAWKEN

aid of Shehawken, kind and true,
I sing a fond farewell,
But, maiden, though I sing adieu,
My love I cannot tell—
My love I cannot tell to thee
For parting gives me pain,
Oh may I in the days to be
Meet with thee once again.

Maid of Shehawken, sweet and fair,
Accept my humble praise,
And may thy path be free from care,
Full happy be thy days,
And ever mid the lure of life
Where e'er thy lot may be,
In pleasant paths or weary strife—
Remember, I love thee.

Maid of Shehawken, kind and true,
Tho' far away we roam,
Few places will we find, O few
As sweet as our highland home,
And tho' Life's pathway lead along
The shining streets of gold,
Our lips will never know a song
As sweet as the songs of old.

Maid of Shehawken, dearer far
Than any that I know,
Lighting my pathway like a star,
Afar from thee I go,
But tho' I leave the Hills of Wayne
My heart is still with thee,
O maiden, may we meet again
In the days that are to be.

TO THE DELAWARE

Cease thy murmuring, Delaware,
For thy many braves so fair
Who are sleeping by thy stream—
Rouse them not—there let them dream.
For upon that silent shore
Indian's cry shall sound no more.
There, where still the owlets cry
And the solemn night-winds sigh,
Let the victor's head remain
With the spirits of the slain,
Leave the warriors fast asleep
Where the willows o'er them weep,
For thy murmuring, Delaware,
Cannot wake those sleeping there,
For thy voice deep in the foam
Cannot ever call them home.

There, where low and high degree
Sleep beneath the self-same tree,
And where warriors small and great,
Share in death a common fate,
Leave the pale-face and the braves
Side by side within their graves.

There, where ridges lifting high
Try to bridge the endless sky,
And where willows bend like lead
O'er the footprints of the dead—
To each brother slumbering there,
Sing sweet songs, my Delaware.

REQUIEM:

Brave!—thy happy days have fled
Into silence with the dead;
Thy canoe, thy well-worn way,
And thy bow are in decay.
And no more thy camp-fires gleam
By thy sweet, complaining stream;

And I mourn thy ruthless fate;
Weeping am I—but too late—
For upon that silent shore
Indian's cry shall sound no more.

STARLIGHT LAKE

Well named thou art, O little lake
Set in among the hills;
Well named art thou,—each star doth make
Reflected forms that fancies wake
And memory fondly fills.

And nightly on the rugged shore
Each cot with ruddy beam
Lights up thy face from pane and door
And throws a stream of silver o'er
Thy bosom like a dream.

Thy hemlock hills, now dimly grown,
Fling shadows on thy face,
And to their branch the birds have flown,
Except the owl, whose monotone
The listening ear can trace.

There, where the starlight thickly trails
A path across thy wave,
A passing boat a boatman hails
Whose maiden crew still softly sails
As with a pilot brave.

While from thy shore a lithe canoe
Shoots o'er thy bosom fair,
Leaving behind a milk-white view
As when the beaver paddled thru
Thy waters unaware.

Up rides the moon with rosy rim
All silently and still,
Chasing away the shadows dim
That on thy surface seem to swim
Like wood nymphs from the hill.

Now midnight comes, and on thy shore
No boatman plies his way,
The cottage lights shine forth no more
From window-pane or open door
Where yet thy shadows play.

Silent and strangely still is all;
The stars like candles are,
No echoes on the forest fall, —
Each lonely owl hath ceas'd to call
His wood-mate from afar.

Silent and calmly still is all;
Dim Night is monarch now,
His kingdom is the midnight air,
The forests his attendants fair,
Who, at his bidding, bow —

And stand like sentinels asleep
Beneath the moon's wan beam,
Until Aurora fair doth creep
Above the hill where she doth keep
Bright morn with welcome gleam.

AN INQUIRY

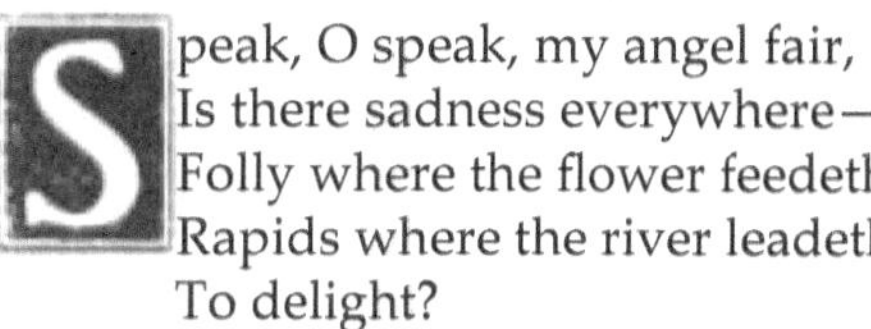peak, O speak, my angel fair,
Is there sadness everywhere—
Folly where the flower feedeth
Rapids where the river leadeth
To delight?

Is there, is there anything
An eternal joy can bring—
What is real and what but seemeth
Like a dream a dreamer dreameth
Thru the night?

Can there be, Angel of Love
Can there be bright homes above—
What is Life—and when it endeth
What is Death—why it descendeth
I implore?

Tell me, Angel, can it be
That thy hand is leading me—
Tell me, are these seraphs singing
Up in heaven, gladness bringing
Evermore?

TWIN LAKE

IN THE WAYNE HIGHLANDS

The shadows fall on Twin Lake fair
As crimson sets the Autumn sun;
A holy hush is on the air
Of eventide and day is done.

No zephyrs kiss the little lake;
So still and calm is either shore,
That on her face dim shadows wake
And deepen ever more and more.

And where the long-leaf laurels grow
A cuckoo sounds the hour of rest,
And fondly answering far below
Its mate is calling from her nest.

Now comes the twilight, calm and still,
And, with a cloak of sable hue,
Half hides the lake and upland hill
That faint and fainter fades from view.

And through the broken web of night
Each stalwart star with even ray
Reflects upon the lake a light
To guide a boatman on his way.

And soon the massive moon doth ride
Athwart the pine trees' heavy shade,
That doth her fiery chariot hide,
As an apparent halt is made.

And sweetly from a maiden fair
In yon canoe that skirts the shore
A laugh rings out upon the air
And echoes softly o'er and o'er

Till dying on the distant hill,
An evening silence settles far, —
A quietness, so calm, so still,
With rising moon and silent star —

That peace, sweet peace subdues the soul,

While on the clear and pensive air
The bells of Como softly toll
The ever-sacred hour of prayer.

THE MAN WHO SWEARS

It is often, yes, often that the man who swears
Is a man who dares and a man who cares;
For the gentle voice and the eye of blue
Will sometimes tell of a heart less true
Than the rough, cold voice and manner stern —
And you some day this truth will learn: —
That often, yes, often that the man who swears
Is a man who dares and a man who cares.

When you are sick with fever and pain,
Who comes to ease your weary brain?
Is it the friend with the eyes of blue
And gentle voice that comes to you,
Or, is it the one with manner cold
And voice so stern and ways so bold,
That presses a hand on your fevered brow
And soothes your troubled spirits now.

When you are down and your friends are few,
Who is it comes to comfort you?
Is it the one with eyes so mild
And voice as sweet as a little child —
Is it the one with gentle way
That comes to you and dares to say: —
So sorry, friend; say, here's my hand,
I'll do your bidding; now just command?

When in misfortune you need a friend
Who will fight for you to the bitter end —
Is it always the one who speaks quite low
And fears to say what he knows, is so,
Or is it the man who speaks his mind
And shows some mettle — and hardly kind
Whose heart is cold until your woe
Melts an entrance as the sun melts snow?

I would not say that swearing is right
But I say some men are willing to fight —
It is wrong indeed for a man to swear,
And I envy no one's weakness there —

Still I believe, with me you would say
While one will swear and another pray
You would follow the man who is willing to dare
Tho one might pray and the other swear.

THE GLEN

ere Nature's nice adjusted tool
Hath cut a chasm; and each pool
Reflects a narrow, rocky room
Where sun-born flowers seldom bloom,
But where the ledging, level shelves
Betray the dance hall of the elves.

And overhead the tasseled trees
Frown from the wall, and with each breeze
Awake the solemn avenue,
But hide from sight the upward view,
When with a hundred harps they sing
To Boreas their mighty king.

Here Echo dwells in lonely mood,
And answers to the dying wood;
Unsuited to a varying rhyme
She hath no voice for tuneful Time
Content to speak as she hath heard
The lyric wind, the singing bird.

Here these same falls awoke the glen
Long, long before the march of men;
Long, long before yon broken soil
Brought forth the fruit of human toil
And here these falls will dance and play
When feeling man has passed away.

Sing little Falls; and echo Glen,
Till silent are the songs of men
And they that dwell upon the earth
Have disappeared as at thy birth
And senseless Rock—if think ye can,
Think ye—how short the life of man!

HOPE

Kind guardian of the Lonely Shore,
And Sorrow's true and only friend,
Comforting angel of the poor—
What heavenly spirit did descend
With passive voice, with ways unknown,
Within thy very self complete?
O Hope, when left at last alone
We fall a suppliant at thy feet
And worship there, with heart forlorn
From childhood's land of make-believe,
Through early youth, the brightening morn,
Till tottering age, the fading eve.

And who could walk without thee, friend?
Who walk dim paths without thy hand?
From out the world shouldst thou ascend
Blind Poverty would stalk the land;
Despair would seize some simple knave
And Hatred every evil one,—
O Hope, for more would seek the grave
Without thy timely vision shown:—
The sick upon the lowly bed;
The blind a-begging as of yore;
The weeping child who works unfed;
The prisoner by the fatal door,
All, led along, still cling below
To feel thy subtle charms so free,
As wearily, drearily on they go,
Following, following after thee.

And when upon Life's field they fall,
When Disappointment reigns supreme,
Thy voice, omnipotent, would call
E'en from the dust their fondest dream;
Would call and wake the slumbering thought,
And point it to some great ideal
While adding all, but taking naught
From out the present, living real.
Then, Hope, thou sentinel of light

By Disappointment's lonely shore,
Speak out amid the depth of night
And guide us safely evermore.

LINES TO LIARS

et lawyers harp about the law,
And all its majesty and might;
They find in every case a flaw
And think -they're right.

Let politicians praise the truth
And laud its virtue to the sky—
They practice from their very youth
To give the lie.

Let prophets send the saints to heaven
And damn poor sinners e'en to hell—
How such authority is given
They cannot tell.

Let doctors prate of human pain
Alleviated by their skill,
When Death's dull sickness comes, in vain
Is every pill.

Let poets pipe of bloody war
And claim its carnal method right;
They're only piping cowards, for
Not one will fight.

And so it seems we mortals boast
Of knowledge where we know the least
And show our ignorance the most
Like any beast.

FOOLING

He was a lad—a tender boy,
And she—she held him as her toy,
And when she wearied of his way
And would with other playthings play,
I heard him say beneath his breath:—
A fool am I; it is my death—
She jilted me—the little lass,—
I will not let such fooling pass
But shift at once some bitter dart
Back—back again into her heart,
But then thought he—All those who play
With fools are fools as well as they,
And so he made a living rule:—
It takes a fool to fool a fool.

Lector House believes that a society develops through a two-fold approach of continuous learning and adaptation, which is derived from the study of classic literary works spread across the historic timeline of literature records. Therefore, we aim at reviving, repairing and redeveloping all those inaccessible or damaged but historically as well as culturally important literature across subjects so that the future generations may have an opportunity to study and learn from past works to embark upon a journey of creating a better future.

This book is a result of an effort made by Lector House towards making a contribution to the preservation and repair of original ancient works which might hold historical significance to the approach of continuous learning across subjects.

HAPPY READING & LEARNING!

LECTOR HOUSE LLP
E-MAIL: lectorpublishing@gmail.com